# LORRIES OF ARABIA 2

# ERF NGC

Robert Hackford

# REVIEWS OF THE FIRST VOLUME

Robert Hackford's genuine passion for this ERF type shines through every page and the book contains many fine and evocative photographs in colour or black and white. I particularly liked the documentation on British hauliers who travelled the desert roads, such as Richard Read and Eric Vick.

**John Henderson,** *Transport News*

*Lorries of Arabia* is insightful, rich in detail and captures the character of a truck that would have been respected as the ERF flagship of its generation, had more been sold in Britain. Only one NGC 420 may remain, but Hackford's book is the next best thing.

**Ed Burrows,** *Trucking*

This new paperback book takes a nostalgic look at the role ERF's world-class long-haul legend, the NGC, played in the transportation of goods across continents during the golden age of the Middle East Run.

*Truck Stop News*

The book is all about the life and times of ERF NGCs in general and about the Middle East examples in particular: what they looked like, how well they performed, where they ventured, what they were like to drive, what they were like to live in and where they stood in ERF's contribution to Britain's place in the history of the TIR trail.

Written with authority by Robert Hackford, the book delves into the trials and traditions of the TIR-trail, and looks at how the hard-working and well-engineered ERF NGC developed its reputation as one of the best trucks for mountain-hauls.

**Andy Stewart,** *Trucking*

Mr Hackford has a very easy to read style of writing that makes the information that is included relatively easy to digest. The book contains plenty of anecdotes from Robert's time on the road and his passion and enjoyment of his time driving trucks is clearly reflected by the way he describes the life of a long-distance lorry driver. The romance of the open road is clearly apparent from Mr Hackford's excellent descriptive writing.

**truckblog.co.uk**

This book would get five stars just for the title. It's well researched, comprehensively illustrated and is essential reading for the many enthusiasts of this golden chapter in haulage history.

*Truck and Driver*

# LORRIES OF ARABIA 2

## ERF NGC

Robert Hackford

Old Pond PUBLISHING

First published 2016

Published by
5M Publishing Ltd,
Benchmark House,
8 Smithy Wood Drive,
Sheffield, S35 1QN, UK
Tel: +44 (0) 1234 81 81 80
www.5mpublishing.com


A catalogue record for this book is available from the British Library

ISBN 978-1-910456-21-7


Book layout by David Exley www.beamreachuk.co.uk
Printed by Replika Press Pvt. Ltd., India.
Photos as credited in the text

# CONTENTS

# ABOUT THE AUTHOR

*(Photo: Gary Corbishley)*

Robert Hackford (born 1952) started out as a school teacher, progressing to a headship quite early on. However, mid-career he opted for change and became a TIR-driver instead. After doing Europe for a while, a trip to Turkey whetted his appetite for long-haul work and he subsequently spent a number of years driving to North Africa. He made a handful of Astran trips to the Arabian Gulf driving a Eurostar with a Twin-splitter, as far afield as Doha in Qatar. For Robert, each new trip was an adventure with a sense of achievement at the end of it. He even ran his own unit and trailer for a while. During the 'Nineties he often wrote articles for the various truck magazines. Robert returned to teaching, first in Istanbul then Rome and eventually in Cairo where he served as the head of a British International school before retiring in 2014. He is the author of *Lorries of Arabia: ERF NGC*, published by Old Pond in 2015.

# ACKNOWLEDGEMENTS

Rik Gruwez: Belgian haulier. Marc Van Steenbergen: Belgian haulier. Mario Maes: Belgian transport historian. Wobbe Reitsma: Dutch transport historian. Barry Randall: ERF archivist. Martin Wilcox: ERF blogger and archivist. Ken Broster: former general manager for Trans Arabia in Jeddah. Marcus Lester: truck photographer. Peter Davies: transport journalist. Niels Jansen: transport journalist. George Starkey: ERF restorer. Ian Tyler: former driver for Cunard Arabian Middle East Lines. Gary Corbishley: restorer and owner of NGC KCH 95N. Rene Postma: erstwhile owner of the same vehicle. Vince Cooke: former NGC driver. Jerry Cooke: former NGC driver and mechanic for Trans Arabia. Ron Hawkins: former NGC driver and mechanic for Trans Arabia. Chris Till: former NGC driver for Eric Vick. Steve Little: former NGC driver for Richard Read. John Heath: former NGC driver for Beresford Transport. Dave Anslow: former NGC driver for Trans Arabia. Bob Jarratt: former NGC driver for PG Horridge. Mike Beard: former fitter for Richard Read.

*(Photo: Marcus Lester)*

# INTRODUCTION

*(Photo: Peter Davies)*

The picture above was taken at the 1974 Earls Court motor show. This ERF NGC had a Cummins 335. At this stage, the NGC was still only an export model as it wasn't offered to UK operators until 1975.

Thanks to ERF archivist Barry Randall, we now know that only 91 ERF NGCs were built in total, but that didn't put me off writing *Lorries of Arabia: ERF NGC*. The publication of that book created quite a lot of interest, stimulating new contributors to bring a wealth of fresh information, stories and pictures into the arena about this fascinating lorry. Having now met a surprising number of drivers who pushed these lorries to their limits in the Middle East it hard to find anyone with a serious complaint against them. These vehicles were very highly regarded indeed by those who used them. At least 31 of them are known either to have worked on the Middle East run or to have worked on the Arabian Peninsula on 'internals': hence this continuation of that theme. Theoretically, there is no reason why all 31 of them couldn't have been in the Middle East at the same point in time – and there may have been more!

This volume continues to explore the fortunes of this legendary ERF. To avoid unnecessary repetition, *Lorries of Arabia 2: ERF NGC* is designed to be a companion to the first book and has a different format, being made up of pictures supported by detailed captions, rather than having a full text supported by pictures.

*(Photo: TRUCK magazine)*

Whilst other British manufacturers, such as Leyland, were producing special, long-haul left-hand-drive versions of domestic models to meet the requirements of Britain's entry into the Common Market during the 1970s, ERF produced the NGC, which was a unique long-hauler designed solely for operation in Europe and the Middle East.

The NGC 'European' (to give it its full name) was only ever built with left-hand drive and nearly all of them were powered by a turbocharged Cummins NTC 335 engine, driving through a Fuller Road-Ranger 9-speed gearbox and a heavy duty Kirkstall D85 hub-reduction 13-tonne axle. Just a handful, however, were equipped with Cummins NTC 290s coupled to 13-speed Fuller 'boxes. The very well-appointed Motor Panels cab is described in some detail in *Lorries of Arabia: ERF*

*NGC.* It could be tilted to 68 degrees and had provision for a roof-mounted air-conditioning unit.

ERF's coding system to describe, for example, the NGC 420 works as follows: N = 7MW 'European' steel cab; G = export special specification cab; C = Cummins; 42 = 42 tonnes GTW; 0 = 4x2 two axle tractive unit or rigid.

Although ERF brochures of the 1970s offered Gardner engines as an option, it is now known from ERF records that no NGC left the factory with a Gardner engine.

*(Photo: Robert Hackford)*

This close-up picture of KCH 95N shows how beautifully Gary Corbishley has restored it.

The superior performance of the NGC was legendary, especially in the mountains, but with escalating fuel costs the comparatively thirsty NTC 335 hastened the NGC's replacement with the more sophisticated LHD B-series ERF in 1977. Built between the beginning of 1973 and the end of 1977 the NGC maintained a small but very special place in the history of the Middle East run, a third of them having performed on the Arabian Peninsula.

This book is about the ERF with the boxy, square-fronted, tall version of the Motor Panels mark 4 cab. This cab was called the 7MW, by ERF. The subject of the round-fronted versions of the fixed metal cab with the split windscreen used by ERF (3MW, 4MW, 5MW, 6MW, etc.) is not within the remit of this work.

*(Photo: Van Steenbergen archives)*

The NGC appears very fleetingly in many transport history books; and it is sometimes missed out altogether, almost as if it were just a transitory stop-gap between the 3MW-cabbed MGC 'European' and the LHD B-series. However, it was clearly nothing of the kind, being, as I see it, a very distinct model in its own right, with its own character and its own components. Given that the B-series was conceived at much the same time as the NGC, one wonders why the tilting 7MW cab was ever introduced, or why the LHD full-height export version of the SP sleeper cab was not introduced in 1974 when the B-series was launched instead of it in 1977. It would have served as a proper Euro-truck with either LHD or RHD (which the NGC didn't, being only LHD).

The NGC, far from being a stop-gap, was conceived and built as a longer-term Euro-truck and was absolutely a model in its own right. The B-series was actually intended to serve as an updated version of the A-series, largely for domestic use. The original B-series was a day-cabbed lorry which was clearly not intended for European work. Nor was it intended to become a sleeper unit, the construction of the day-cab mitigating against such a development. Even the chassis was not long enough to accommodate a sleeper. On the other hand, the NGC was a premium Euro-truck developed at considerable cost almost simultaneously with the inception of the B-series project. When one looks at the comparatively low-power engines utilised, these early B-series units were quite clearly A-series replacements, rather than NGC-series replacements. Even the early B-series exports to Belgium and Holland were flat-top domestic Jennings conversions with LHD. It is no coincidence that the NGC was discontinued in 1977 just as the new LHD European sleeper version of the B-series was introduced.

Apparently, the new Euro-spec B-series was pushed to the fore by ERF at this point, leaving us to wonder just how many NGCs might have been sold if production had continued. Bill Fitzsimons, a former ERF engineer who occasionally used to attend to the Trans Arabia fleet in Jeddah, recalls that that the NGC was one of the finest machines ERF ever built; and that ERF could, in his opinion, have sold hundreds of them if they hadn't been pushing the new B-series Euro-truck sales so hard. I showed in *Lorries of Arabia* that drivers generally preferred the NGC to the B-series. However, it is known that the B-series proved more frugal than the NGC, which probably accounts for the progression. Ironically, that same fuel-efficient, Euro-friendly version of the 14-litre Cummins utilised by the B-series – the NTE 290 – was tried and tested in an NGC belonging to Cummins itself (see below).

Bearing in mind that the Vijore NGCs gave several years of trouble-free service on the gruelling Middle East run, fitting a Cummins E290 and creating a right-hand-drive version might have extended the existence of this flagship long-hauler, but in doing so ERF would have had to continue outsourcing its cab manufacture to Motor Panels of Coventry.

It was entirely fitting that Cummins of New Malden should have this 1974 ERF NGC to haul its hospitality trailer to transport events. For a start, unlike other ERF models, NGCs were only fitted with Cummins engines even though others were offered. HNV 59N

*(Photo: Marcus Lester)*

(chassis no. 29069) also doubled up as a test bed for the new big-cam Cummins 290. An NTC E290, coupled with a 9-speed Fuller, was fitted to the very last NGC to leave the production line, for Falcon Freight in Jeddah on 22 December 1977 (chassis no. 31927). Had this been fitted wholesale to ERF NGCs, it would have replaced the all-American NTC 335 power-units and would possibly have given the NGC a new lease of life.

*(Photo: Marcus Lester)*     *(Photo: Mick Jones)*

HNV 59N subsequently passed on to Pountains Heavy Haulage of Sudbury, then to Redcap Transport of Newport. It was photographed still intact in 1994, sold on for restoration in 1997 but scrapped in 2003. Mick Jones took the second picture when he transported away the remains after it had been dismantled.

The picture left shows Peter Foden, managing director of ERF Ltd of Sandbach, examining a new NGC. In the July 1975 issue of *TRUCK* magazine, a letter appeared from him with some interesting and revealing comments on the previous month's

Euro Test in which the NGC had excelled itself. His letter ran as follows:

I enjoyed reading your Euro-Test report in the June issue of TRUCK, and we are all pleased that our vehicle matched favourably with the best of the European competition. It must be remembered that the model was introduced some two years ago and is due to be replaced by the B-series with the SP cab early next year. However, the proven major components are unlikely to be changed radically, and I think the concept of picking the best components and staying with them is right.

We feel that we still have some way to go to make the ideal truck, but the improvements that are coming along in the pipeline will, I believe, give our competitors something to think about. I am only sorry that the present depressed state of the European truck market has prevented us from selling more vehicles into Europe, but I hope operators there will now realise that a British manufacturer is serious about Europe.

Parts and service arrangements for British trucks travelling through Europe have always been questioned by operators. We, at ERF, are in the process of extending our service network across Europe to the Middle East markets.

In the event, it was a further two years before the B-series actually replaced the NGC; and even if the B-series was destined at this stage to do so, the NGC remained a distinct model in its own right.

| Truck | Av speed(kph) | %rating |
|---|---|---|
| FIAT 170/35 | 63.63 | 100 |
| ERF NGC420 | 62.87 | 98.8 |
| FORD HA4234 | 62.15 | 97.6 |
| ERF 40.C2 (B) | 61.99 | 97.4 |
| SCANIA LB111.02 | 61.84 | 97.1 |
| FORD HA4231 | 61.19 | 96.1 |
| BEDFORD TM3800 | 60.62 | 95.2 |
| MAN 19.320 | 60.61 | 95.1 |
| M BENZ 1932 | 60.14 | 94.5 |
| MAGIRUS 310D16 | 59.68 | 93.7 |
| VOLVO F89 | 59.46 | 93.4 |
| SAVIEM SM340 | 59.32 | 93.2 |
| SCANIA LB140 (V8) | 59.19 | 93.0 |
| MAN 19.280 | 59.06 | 92.8 |
| BERLIET TR320 | 57.94 | 91.0 |
| LEYLAND MTC3832 | 57.60 | 90.5 |
| DAF FT2800DKS7 | 56.65 | 89.0 |

This table is from the Euro Test conducted by *TRUCK* magazine in July/August 1977. The ERF NGC wasn't in the test because the new Euro-spec B-series had taken over, but the editor Pat Kennett saw fit to include the previous Euro Test speed records round the gruelling Ardennes route. The NGC's position near the top, beating everything but the Fiat, including the new B-series, just shows what a formidable opponent it would still have been if it had remained in production beyond 1977.

Pat Kennett wrote:

Since the first Supertest, when we ran the steel-cab Cummins 335 ERF which did so well for itself and upheld Britain's honours in the battle field, the Sandbach independent has revised its whole model range to what is known as the B-series.

*(Photo: Marcus Lester)*

In his magnanimous review of *Lorries of Arabia* in the Summer 2015 issue of *TRUCKING* magazine, Ed Burrows wondered if 'the unavailability of a LHD option may have been a factor in the low take-up of NGCs in the UK'. This is a fair point, if only because a left-hand-drive ERF with a history of Middle East work would not have held a high re-sale value in the '70s. But his comment also begs the question: would a RHD version of the NGC have sold well in Britain? We'll never know, of course, but a high proportion of British-registered long-haul trucks in those days had RHD.

Which brings me to the subject of the only ERF with a 7MW cab to end up with right-hand drive, as far as I know. UGE 852R, chassis 33315, was a hybrid beast. It wasn't an NGC at all, but a right-hand-drive 6x4 MDC 852 which had its set-back 6MW cab replaced by a 7MW cab when Cossington Commercials fitted a Cummins 350 lump into it during its time with Pountains Heavy Haulage. It originally had a Cummins 335 and a Fuller RTO915 gearbox. Eventually this vehicle passed to J. & Y. Weir of Fernigait in Scotland, where it hauled heavy loads internally on the Ravenscraig site at Motherwell.

*(Photo: Author's collection)*

This breakdown wagon was operated by Reliable Recovery Services of London on trade plates. It was later registered Q824 RGC and was operated by BFI Recovery Services.

# A FINE EXAMPLE IN PRESERVATION

*(Photo: Marcel Eyckmans)*

Much was written about this Cummins 335-powered NGC in *Lorries of Arabia*. It was supplied new to Eyckmans of Betekom in Belgium as 4x2 tractive unit, then later acquired a Fassi crane and Hendrickson double-drive. Thus enlarged, it was employed in the woods on round timber work. Marcel Eyckmans originally planned to restore it himself and after spraying it with grey primer he stored it for 17 years. Rene Postma, a Dutch transport historian, then acquired it in 2003 but later sold it on. It is now preserved by Gary Corbishley of Lower Loxley and it is probably the only remaining ERF NGC still running. In service, it ran as a 6x4 tractive unit hauling a round timber trailer but in the following pictures it is seen as a ballasted tractor.

My suspicion that KCH 95N actually left ERF with a 9-speed Fuller gearbox turned out to be well founded. Despite having entered service (as 7DF 44) with Eyckmans in Belgium as new with a 13-speed Fuller gearbox, it is now known to have left the factory in Sandbach on 24 May 1974 with a Fuller RT 9509A gearbox (although the build card stated 9508A for some reason). Rene Postma was able to pick up the tale and informed me that on 31 May, Mr W. Ghys of CDB (Cummins Distribution Belgium) visited Marcel Eyckmans to discuss the purchase of an NGC 420. On 4 June Mr Eyckmans was offered one and the Fuller

RTO 9513 was offered for an extra 15,000 Belgium franks, which carried a one-year warranty or 80,000 kms, whichever came first.

*(Photo: Robert Hackford)*

The driving position is very comfortable, with excellent forward vision. Some drivers found the NGC more comfortable to drive than the later B-series. They also preferred its superior performance on the road. Operators, however, found the B-series more frugal and, of course, the cab was a more sophisticated living space. I had the honour of parading KCH 95N round the arena at the 2015 Kelsall ERF gathering, and personally, I think the driving position in the NGC is superb. I have to say, the sound of the Cummins 335 sounded wonderful as I accelerated from the point where the MC describes each vehicle!

Gary Corbishley at the wheel of his restored NGC on a run through the Staffordshire countryside. It was generally agreed among

*(Photo: Robert Hackford)*

drivers that the NGC was a lovely truck to drive. Jack Cooke, ERF's chief engineer who designed the 7MW, told a *Motor Transport* reporter in 1977: 'From the outset, the 7MW was virtually trouble-free, and there are not many trucks you can say that about.'

*(Photo: Robert Hackford)*

This shows the leaf-springs supported by KCH's Hendrickson rear bogie. The bogie was transplanted from a White tractive unit in Belgium when the truck was about four years old.

On the standard 4x2 tractive units, excellent stability was achieved by an over-slung rear spring arrangement. Specially designed supple and strong leaf springs of extra length gave first-class ride characteristics, whilst double acting telescopic shock absorbers were standard on both axles.

Vehicle restoration requires commitment. Here, Gary Corbishley dusts off KCH 95N's front grille in the workshop before departing for the 2012 Kelsall truck show.

*(Photo: Robert Hackford)*

*(Photo: Robert Hackford)*

The Motor Panels mark 4 cab was very well appointed in the ERF 7MW, with double bunks and a host of refinements not normally found in British trucks of the period. However, a glance at this picture shows how much glass there was in the rear half of the cab, which means

*(Photo: Rene Postma)*

that winter nights would have been a challenge, especially as effective night-heaters hadn't yet been fully developed and were not widely available. Some drivers, such as Steve Little who drove for Richard Read, lined the glass to the rear of the driver for better insulation.

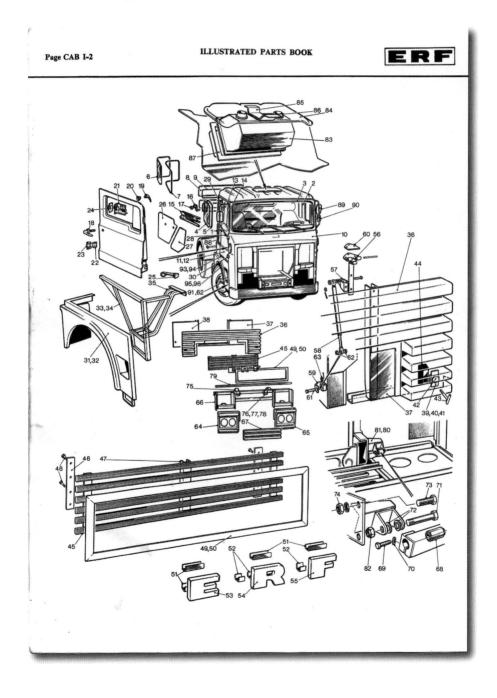

# ERF NGCS AT WORK IN EUROPE

© Peter J Davies

In this evocative photo the low sunlight picks out the features of the Motor Panels cab of a French NGC parked in a UK services area. The existence of this lorry was one of several recent discoveries since the first book. Another of these is the British-operated unit registered HMO 220N, which was operated by Calor Transport and was subject to tanker regulations. It is quite possible that Calor ran more than one of these and it is also known that at least one 5MW-cabbed unit was supplied to them. An ERF demonstrator, supplied to S. Jones for an equipment exhibition, was written off in an accident on the way to the event. A revised register of ERF NGCs can be found at the end of this volume.

The French ERF advert shows a 1974 NGC registered 7011-KG-78, which was operated by Mentre of Yvelines.

In an article, Derek Bill, ERF's export sales manager, told *Commercial Motor* magazine (12 May 1984): 'We've developed a policy of concentrating on certain specific markets. We are not GM or Ford. We can't spread our wings all over the world.'

So in the '60s and '70s ERF tried France, The Netherlands and Switzerland but especially targeted Belgium, working through Cummins Distributor Belgium (CDB) in Brussels. But by the end of the '70s ERF wound up its European operations, having sold only a couple of hundred or so vehicles. Derek Bill explained that ERF's Euro-trucks had been expensive to build: 'Their specification was so dissimilar. We were 32-tonners with right-hand drive while they were mostly 38-tonners with left-hand drive. Therefore we had to produce separate vehicles in low volumes – not a profitable exercise.'

The Europe project ended with LHD B-series ERFs. Thereafter, the LHD C-series was marketed in the Arabian Gulf where it sold well. It wasn't until the early '90s, when the EU borders melted, that ERF renewed its European attempts with the LHD E-series and later the EC-series.

*(Photo: Niels Jansen)*

*(Photo: Van Steenbergen archives)*

Van Steenbergen of Arendonk in Belgium ran six 335-powered ERF NGCs largely on European tilt work. They also had two left-hand-drive B-series ERFs. Marc Van Steenbergen informed me that the reason for purchasing the ERFs was that in the 1960s and 1970s they ran German Krupps, having about 15 of them with Cummins V8 engines; and that the Belgian importer of Krupp started to import ERF from 1973. This importer in Brussels was CDB (Cummins Distributor

Belgium) from whom they also bought White and Autocar tractive units. Van Steenbergen was actually an ERF dealer during the time that they ran their NGCs. On one occasion, an Eric Vick NGC appeared on the premises for minor repairs whilst on long-haul work. An ERF sign hung outside the offices, along with a Krupp sign.

This picture shows AFU 615, Van Steenbergen's fleet number 28, later 31, which is now known to have had a Cummins 335 with a Fuller RTO 9095A gearbox. An interior picture of the cab featured in ERF's own *Chassis* magazine shows the gear-knob

*(Photo: Van Steenbergen archives)*

to be of the chrome-topped 'bicycle-bell' design shared, incidentally, by the 9-speed Fullers fitted in the six VIJORE NGCs.

Its chassis number was 22993 and it was the first NGC built, having been exhibited at the Brussels motor show in January 1973. Marc Van

Steenbergen informed me that their early NGCs suffered from windscreen wiper failure until ERF beefed up the triple wiper mechanism, and sure enough, the picture shows the nearside wiper missing! One correspondent reports that Van Steenbergen's chief mechanic, Gustav Vanherck, informed him that the ERF NGCs had been good lorries to work on, and as reported elsewhere in this book, were reliable but prone to water-pump failures.

More information has come to light about the second NGC, also shown at Brussels in 1973. This was registered in Belgium as JJ393 and operated by Thibault of Stree. It was a draw-bar outfit (chassis number 24684; engine number 51900) with a Cummins NTC 335 and a Fuller RTO 9509A gearbox. It acquired an Atelier Leone tipper body and initially pulled a MOL trailer, after which it pulled a LAG trailer.

*(Photo: Mario Maes collection)*

This rather charming picture shows a young Belgian driver, Marino Moerman, with his ERF NGC. The company is Bertrand Gruwez of Brugge (Bruges), who were heavy haulage contractors. They later had a B-series unit.

In *TRUCK* magazine, January 1976, the editor wrote a piece looking back at the highlights of the previous year. About the ERF NGC he had this to say:

> In midsummer we went all foreign, or at least European and staged the first of our series of European Supertests over a tough special route in Belgium. One of Europe's smallest but most successful manufacturers ERF, put their money where their mouth was and took on the might of the continent. No-

one was more surprised than us when their Cummins 335 powered European thrashed the entire opposition in terms of journey times, turned in very respectable economy and proved to be the most versatile when it came to coupling to various different trailers.

*(Photo: Wobbe Reitsma collection)*

*(Photo: Niels Jansen)*

A number of NGCs saw service with Dutch operators. These two entered service in 1976 with Rien de Vos of Goudswaard near Rotterdam. They were registered 83-75-HB and 21-96-HB. Hauling brick trailers equipped with cranes, they covered the first 400,000 kms with no trouble, and were withdrawn in 1979. Rien De Vos also ran three LHD B-series ERF units with Jennings conversion sleeper cabs.

*(Photo: Marcus Lester)*

*(Photo: Wobbe Reitsma collection)*

Bought new by Kooij of Hendrik-Ido-Ambacht, Holland in 1974, DB-77-52 passed to Cess Willem-stein, of Barendrecht, in 1978. This NGC 420 had a turbocharged Cummins 335 engine and Fuller 9-speed 'box. DB-77-52 was in the colours of HT Wilhelminakade of Rotterdam with a little added fantasy. It remained in service for 15 years until October 1989, when it was sold to a vehicle breaker, with high mileage on the clock.

*(Photo: Wobbe Reitsma collection)*

16-37-FB entered service in Holland in 1975 with Groen of Nieuw Lekkerland, with whom it served until 1982. Typically, ERF NGCs gave at least seven years of service in arduous conditions and considerably longer on domestic work.

When Pat Kennett pitted an ERF NGC against several other European trucks in *TRUCK* magazine's Euro Test in 1975, he described the unit as 'king of the mountains' and it held the hill-climbing speed record for some time. Three years later in July 1978, the Volvo F12 was tested around *TRUCK*'s gruelling Ardennes route with the following observation: 'It is no surprise that the F12 set the fastest hill climb aggregate times of any truck of the 22 we've Euro-tested, although the old Cummins 335 European ERF, the first machine we tested in the series, comes close.' Praise indeed!

*(Photo: Peter Davies)*

ERF NGCs registered in the UK were something of a rarity, most of them having been exported to the Continent. The Scottish firm Greer of Holytown ran this NGC registered GDS 543N. Closer inspection of this picture reveals traditional 'lining out' of the panels by a skilled sign-writer. Even the air foils either side of the windscreen have been decorated.

So what were the other British-built (or British-assembled) LHD tractive units available in the mid-'70s equipped with that combination of Cummins NTC 335 engine and 9-speed Fuller gearbox? Well, there appear only to be four others: rare examples of ERF's own 5MW-cabbed 'European', rare examples of the Seddon-Atkinson 400, rare examples of the Ford Transcontinental and rare examples of the Leyland Marathon.

*(Photo: Geoff Luther)*

The picture shows driver Bob Jarrett with KRH 153P operated by P.G. Horridge of Poole on European work. Another driver called Dave spoke very highly of this machine and was quoted in *Lorries of Arabia*.

However, I have since spoken to Bob Jarrett, who described this unit as being 'a bit of beast'! At some time in its life it had been fitted with a Cummins 350 from a heavy plant machine, a back-to-front 13-speed Fuller 'box and the rear differential from a coach, giving it phenomenal speed on the straight but taking away its advantage on the hills.

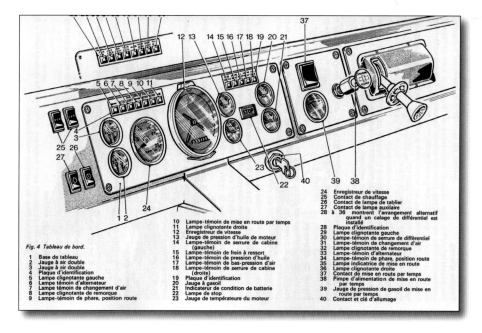

*Fig. 4 Tableau de bord.*

1 Base de tableau
2 Jauge à air double
3 Jauge à air double
4 Plaque d'identification
5 Lampe clignotante gauche
6 Lampe témoin d'alternateur
7 Lampe témoin de changement d'air
8 Lampe clignotante de remorque
9 Lampe-témoin de phare, position route
10 Lampe-témoin de mise en route par temps
11 Lampe clignotante droite
12 Enregistreur de vitesse
13 Jauge de pression d'huile de moteur
14 Lampe-témoin de serrure de cabine (gauche)
15 Lampe-témoin de frein à ressort
16 Lampe-témoin de pression d'huile
17 Lampe-témoin de bas-pression d'air
18 Lampe-témoin de serrure de cabine (droite)
19 Plaque d'identification
20 Jauge à gasoil
21 Indicaterur de condition de batterie
22 Lampe de stop
23 Jauge de température du moteur
24 Enregistreur de vitesse
25 Contact de chauffage
26 Contact de lampe de tablier
27 Contact de lampe auxiliaire
28 à 36 montrent l'arrangement alternatif quand un calage de différentiel est installé
28 Plaque d'identification
29 Lampe clignotante gauche
30 Lampe-témoin de serrure de différentiel
31 Lampe-témoin de changement d'air
32 Lampe clignotante de remorque
33 Lampe-témoin d'alternateur
34 Lampe-témoin de phare, position route
35 Lampe indicatrice de mise en route
36 Lampe clignotante droite
37 Contact de mise en route par temps
38 Pimpe d'alimentation de mise en route par temps
39 Jauge de pression de gasoil de mise en route par temps
40 Contact et clé d'allumage

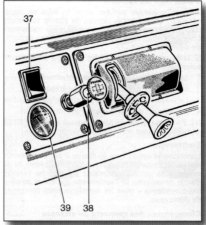

These details from the driver's handbook show the general layout of the dashboard, the switch for engaging the diff-lock and the Cummins priming pump positioned next to the hand-brake.

This Dutch NGC, registered 84-56-JB, was pictured in *Lorries of Arabia* in the livery of Schaap with its pre-registration plate, X-03-44. However, Ben Schaap also ran it in the livery of Konig, as shown in this picture. Unusually, this unit has a roof-rack – the only one I've seen on an NGC. It was the first ERF in Holland to run on ADR plates for hazardous goods. One can almost hear the skeletal structure of tilt boards and drop-sides rattle, as this

*(Photo: Ben Schaap)*

majestic ERF swings into a wet cobbled byway of Holland's industrial heartland; and hear too the crackle of exhaust ricochet among canalside warehouses as the big Cummins pulls straight the heavy equipage to tackle the rise.

# ERF NGCS ON THE MIDDLE EAST RUN

Although much was written about the Vick/Read/Jones NGCs on the Middle East run in *Lorries of Arabia,* more material continues to come to light.

## Three into one for Middle East

THREE hauliers have joined forces and started a new company to carry out a long-term contract to the Middle East.

The new company, Vijor International, will be transporting animal feed mills, in sections, to the Middle East. It was formed by two Gloucestershire operators, Eric Vick Transport of Hardwicke and Richard Read Transport of Longhope, and Cheshire operator Jones Transport of Sandbach.

Eighty-four loads will be delivered in all and the first consignments have already left Britain in convoy. Each 7,000-mile trip will take about a month, but if documentation en route goes smoothly the journey is expected to take only 12 days each way.

The vehicles, derivatives of the ERF European tractive units, are being compelled to detour through the Turkish mountains because the border between Syria and Iraq is closed due to a dispute.

This diversion means that the 42,000kg (41.3-ton) units are travelling over unmetalled roads and are camping in convoy to reduce the risk of theft.

The vehicles have Dynair fans and Jacobs brakes, and the cabs are fitted with air conditioning, refrigerators, cooking units and double bunks.

*(Commercial Motor, 31 October 1975)*

*(Photo: Chris Till)*

The cutting above describes the animal-feed mill that was to be transported piece by piece to Baghdad on these lorries. In the picture, KFH 248P and KFH 249P in Eric Vick livery, along with KFH 250P and KFH 251P in Richard Read livery, are seen here ready for the Baghdad contract. The second picture shows the Eric Vick pair in front of the completed mill in Baghdad.

Two others were painted in the livery of VIJORE. This was the name given to the consortium of hauliers who ran this Middle East operation: Eric Vick, Richard Read and Tony Jones. Most of the work went to Baghdad, but these lorries went variously to Iran, Iraq, Jordan, Saudi Arabia, Turkey, Syria, Qatar and even Pakistan.

If I really had to name favourites from all the known NGCs, I would probably choose the Eric Vick pair. They were quintessential ERF 'Middle Easters' with their roof-mounted air-cons, traditional livery, sun-visors and bumper legends (UK–Middle East). Both of them ended up look-

*(Photo: Ashley Coghill collection)*

ing equally resplendent in the livery of Trans Arabia in Jeddah. To clinch it, they had that fantastic combination of Cummins 335 and 9-speed Fuller. They were registered KFH 248P and 249P, becoming Trans Arabia no. 142 and no. 143 respectively.

The front end of the NGC caused a bit of tutting in the early days as it bore more than a passing resemblance to that of one of its contemporaries, the Scania 140, earning it the nickname of 'Sandbach Scania'. However, we know from *TRUCK* magazine's 1975 Euro Test that the 'Sandbach Scania' actually out-performed the 'Sodertalje ERF' on a demanding route through the Ardennes in Belgium.

When I wondered why I had no pictures of an ERF NGC with a Scania 140 next to it, Ted, an old Eric Vick driver, replied, 'Twas said they only ever saw the Swedish models in their mirrors!'

*(Photo: Chris Till)*

Here is a rare historical glimpse of KFH 249P and its driver, Chris Till, on the first trip VIJORE made out to Baghdad. It shows the cab without its Kysor air-conditioning unit and the trailer without its belly tank. Chris remembers pulling that VIJORE trailer only on the first trip, after which it was either Eric Vick or rental tilts.

*(Photo: Jeff Johnson)*

Although none too clear, this photo shows another NGC at work on Arabian sands! Eric Vick's KFH 248P is parked in a line of other 'Middle Easters' on the dockside at Tartus in Syria, waiting for the ferry to Volos in Greece. The three DAFs in the line belonged to other British companies on Middle East work, Davies Turner, and Whittle. Tartus wasn't the only Syrian port the Eric Vick ERF drivers shipped through: sometimes they used Lattakia.

Drivers who did this work will have little trouble remembering that olfactory cocktail of diesel, urine, rubbish fires, fish and outdoor cooking to be inhaled on Arab docksides; and the omnipresent rumble of engines running on fast tick-over to keep the batteries interested.

The picture shows Chris Till in front of KFH 249P. When I met Chris he was still enthusiastic about this NGC after forty years! He drove it for Eric Vick on Middle East work and he told me that apart from a problem once with the Dynair fan, that lorry never broke down in the five years he drove it. Apparently,

*(Photo: Chris Till collection)*

*(Photo: Chris Till)*

Eric Vick and Richard Read kept on top of the maintenance after every single trip. One of the fitters for Richard Read at the time, Mike Beard, told me that those NGCs were so reliable they only required routine maintenance between big trips.

KFH 249P is seen at rest here on Middle East work with one of Vick's A-series ERFs behind.

The trailer boxes on one side contained cooking equipment and on the other side they contained all manner of spares, including a tow bar and a mono-leaf spring.

Long-haulers will recognise the scenario: piece of waste ground, perhaps a sign saying TIR PARKING, tyres caked in mud from yesterday's arrival in the rain, tilt leaning to one side in a pothole, sunlight fierce, front grille open for shade, trailer box open, folding stools out, kettle beginning to steam, distant sound of the midday call to prayer, rumble of a nearby engine, the presence of dust, faint odours of cooking gas and diesel ...

*(Photo: Chris Till)*

When the VIJORE group first started on Middle East work in 1975, the lorries had to cross some quite demanding terrain, including an unmade military road to Mardin. On the hairpin bends, boys would stand with rocks threatening to smash the windscreen if cigarettes were not thrown out to them. This is well documented in many accounts of Middle East work at that time. The wire-mesh stone guards fitted to the windscreen can be clearly seen in this photograph of KFH 249P about to enter hazardous territory. They were secured at the bottom to the two grab-hands on top of the grille. In order to see more clearly, the drivers cut small holes out of the wire using pliers from the ERF tool-kit.

Also notable is the cover for the Kysor air-conditioner when not in use. The Kysor on this particular vehicle was given a strong frame to sit on, to stop it sagging. Weight was a problem and the Trans Arabia NGCs were given scaffolding-props to hold them up. Richard Read driver Steve Little informed me that they had big aircraft-style swivelling nozzles attached to the vent pipes, the bore of which was apparently just sufficient to stow a can of Coke for cool refreshment.

Drivers reported that ERF NGCs performed very well in snow, especially with snow-chains on. The diff-lock helped, of course.

VIJORE loads outbound included industrial equipment, drill-compressors and sweet wrappers to Baghdad. Sometimes return loads were picked up in Tur-

*(Photo: Chris Till)*

key, or even Austria from where chip-board would be collected. However, return loads such as dates from Iraq were arranged by agents. Another favourite back-load was empty nylon spools from Baghdad to ICI in Pontypool. Even Richard Read's refrigerator trailer made trips out to Baghdad.

Turkey could be horrendous in winter. Chris Till had jack-knifed in appalling conditions and the resulting fairly light damage to the rear of the cab and one of the trailer side-boards can be seen here. The trailer board was straightened out by running over it with the lorry!

*(Photo: Chris Till)*

*(Photo: Chris Till)*

The Ford Transcontinental had belonged to a sub-contractor, Ivor Neil, but it was eventually acquired by Eric Vick. It is interesting to note that the ERF stands at a similar height.

Before the arrival of the NGCs, a demonstrator arrived, which Chris Till drove. Eric Vick apparently sat in it, walked round it, commented that the exhaust pipe looked as if it would need a chimney-sweep's brush to clean it and that was that! Chris and Steve Little maintained that Eric Vick was excellent to work for: very fair, never bore a grudge and ran a good fleet. Once, Eric Vick rode shot-gun in one of his lorries down to the Middle East to see for himself what difficulties the drivers encountered.

Drivers of the VIJORE ERFs tended not to stop at Londra-camp in Istanbul, but preferred to use the Harem Hotel TIR-parking in the Selimiye district on the other side of the Bosphorous. Like Londra-camp it was a very popular watering hole for European drivers heading for the Orient: a veritable truckers' caravanserai where news of the road could be exchanged over a glass or six of Efes pils and a kebab.

KFH 249P is seen in the centre of the first picture (overleaf), which was taken from the Harem Hotel. With it can be seen a DOW Freight trailer and an Eric Vick A-series ERF which had a 250 Cummins, Jake Brake, air-con and a full sleeper-cab conversion.

*(Photo: Chris Till)*

*(Photo: Chris Till)*

In the second picture, also taken from the Harem, both Eric Vick ERF NGCs can be seen with tilts, along with a Richard Read NGC pulling a refrigerated trailer *en route* to Baghdad. With them is an Oryx Volvo F89, also heading for the Middle East. In the foreground are elderly Fiats and a Barrieros Dodge.

I took this picture only a couple of years after the Vick NGCs were sold to Trans Arabia in Jeddah. It shows a wintry view from the parking area back towards the Harem Hotel, and the distinctive slender brown and cream minaret of the mosque next door can be seen against the backdrop of the imposing Selimiye barracks.

*(Photo: Robert Hackford)*

*(Photo: Chris Till)*

This superb picture, showing KFH 248P and KFH 249P, was also taken at the Harem truck stop. The driver having his boots cleaned is David Cleat, who was driving 248P at the time. Turkish TIR-parks tended to be Aladdin's caves for shopping. Chris Till once bought an air horn from the Harem, that blasted out four notes all at once, but he discovered that if used too enthusiastically the ensuing loss of air would cause the trailer brakes to come on.

*(Photo: Chris Till)*

ERF NGC meets camel in the desert. One of the drawbacks of the otherwise well-appointed 7MW cab was that air was sucked in under the doors, which in the desert meant everything in the cab became coated with fine dust.

Routes varied. Sometime the Eastern Bloc was traversed using Czechoslovakia, Hungary, Romania, Bulgaria, Turkey and Iraq. Or the Yugoslavia route was used. One of the most unusual cross-Channel routes was a one-off trip from King's Lynn to Hamburg. Ferries carrying imported cars used to return to the Continent empty, so Eric Vick put a lorry on it, but an alternative return route had to be found, so the scheme was abandoned.

*(Photo: Chris Till)*

When permits got a bit short, lorries were put on the train from Köln to Munich. Chris Till's ERF can be seen here on the train before departure. He recounted an occasion when the drivers had repaired to the station bar and when they emerged they found that the train had left, so they panicked, thinking that they had missed it. As it turned out, it had been shunted into a siding to let another train pass. An interesting detail in this picture is the wire-mesh stone guards fixed across the double headlamps.

On the subject of trains, Chris remembered racing double-headed steam trains down the Ankara to Aksaray road, both lorries and locomotives blasting their horns in defiance, their drivers waving to each other in challenge. Anyone who has driven on that road will know it goes as straight as an arrow across the salt flats.

*(Photo: Chris Till)*

This is another shot of KFH 249P on the train. It clearly shows the huge belly tank for diesel under the trailer (I used to find those belly tanks a great comfort when the running tank was getting a bit low in the wilds). Chris recounts a tale of being stopped at the Saudi border for the usual load inspection. The crane wasn't man enough to lift the load from the deck so that the customs personnel could see underneath, and it was looking as if several days could be lost. So Chris got his tool-kit out and dropped the belly tank onto the ground so that the inspectors could examine the trailer from underneath. This saved the day.

In this picture both KFH 248P and KFH 249P are seen together, and at the far end is a Mercedes LPS driven by Neil Mattley, who (quite sensibly, in my opinion) later became an ERF NGC driver. The Merc ran into trouble after Istanbul and Chris Till attached a bar to the

*(Photo: Chris Till)*

front and towed it some considerable distance to where they could have it repaired. Going up Bolu Mountain, a long steep climb by any standards, they still passed everything, the big Cummins-powered ERF simply storming up the hill. Alarmingly, once on the straight again, Turkish 'Tonka' trucks would overtake the Merc and then try to force themselves into the tiny gap where the tow bar was, to avoid oncoming traffic.

It is often thought that Eric Vick's lorries went to North Africa. However, it was the wagons of another Gloucestershire haulier, C.W. Vick – no relation – that went to Morocco on a contract for Lister engines.

The picture in the Bandag tyres advert was actually taken by Chris Till and here is the photo he took. Chris had nothing but praise for this excellent machine, and one of the things he picked out was the quality of its mirrors, which were very good for the period. Another thing was the trailer handbrake

*(Photo: Chris Till)*

in the cab, which he reckons saved his life on at least one occasion. Anyone who has driven an artic with this feature would probably agree with him (I certainly appreciated it on the series 2 Scanias).

Another strong point on the NGC was a well-installed 9-speed Fuller gearbox. Some NGCs had the round gear-knob with the range-change switch jubilee-clipped to the stick, but those ERFs supplied to VIJORE had the chrome-topped 'bicycle-bell' version.

*(Photo: Chris Till)*

Tipping in the Middle East. Always the dust, the heat and the flies. And always people coming and going – selling things, offering services, wanting to chat. Other ERF NGC drivers on VIJORE work included Keith Burson, Neil Matley, Terry Fit, Chris Morrison, Steve Little and Bob Saunders. There was also Graham Petti-grew, with a reputation for being a very knowledgeable fitter when it came to NGCs.

The breather pipes can clearly be seen. In fact, only six known NGCs were retro-fitted with external breather pipes: KFH 248/249/250/251, GEH 513N and JLG 35N. The pipes were braced to the rear of the cab and tilted with it.

Here is a dramatic view of an ERF NGC storming across Arabia, driven by Keith Burson. KFH 251P, in Richard Read livery, is seen crossing the desert on its way to Baghdad. It was powered by a Cummins 335 with a Fuller 9-speed 'box. It is followed by a Read A-series ERF with a Jennings sleeper pod.

*(Photo: Phil Read collection)*

Keith is quoted in *Beyond the Bosphorus* by Dave Bowers, in which he recounts a tale of having put his powerful ERF to good use, towing an overloaded Turkish tanker up the dreaded road across the Toros Mountains to clear the way for fellow Middle East drivers following in his wake.

Many of the ERF NGCs on Middle East work were fitted with Kysor roof-mounted air-conditioning units. The brochure cover shows a typical '70s unit. The NGC's Motor Panels cab was constructed to accept these units for long-haul work.

NFH 120P: This NGC started life in VIJORE colours and was subsequently painted in Richard Read livery while it was still on Middle East work.

*(Photos: Marcus Lester)*

It was the only one of the six to have an NTC 290 with a 13-speed Fuller 'box, the others all being equipped with NTC 335s and 9-speed Fullers.

Pete Robson drove VIJORE's PDF 444R all the way to Karachi in Pakistan and back via the Khyber Pass in Afghanistan. One can imagine the thundering Cummins NTC 335 as he climbed to the Pakistani border. He stopped, incidentally, to take photos at the pass; and he took the smaller picture shown here, inside Pakistan: his lorry is visible behind the carts. The other two pictures show the lorry in VIJORE livery and in the subsequent livery of Shamara of Southampton.

*(Photo: Pete Robson)*    *(Photo: Marcus Lester collection)*

*(Photo: Marcus Lester)*

When it came off Middle East work this vehicle was driven by Steve Little, who had done some Middle East trips for VIJORE, variously driving an A-series ERF and a day-cabbed Seddon. He told me that typically he'd pick up twenty tonnes of steel in Monmouth and storm past everything over Symonds Yat on the A40 with that NGC. The amount of glass area in the 7MW has been commented on before, and Steve was not alone in finding this a nuisance in winter, so he lined all the glass behind the driver with quilting on the inside for better insulation.

*(Photo: author's collection)*

*(Photo: Marcus Lester)*

KFH 251P hauling a domestic flatbed trailer, but still wearing the trappings of its Middle East service. In the second picture KFH 251P is seen parked next to NFH 120P, having been converted by Richard Read to right-hand drive and given a B-series day-cab.

*(Photos: Marcus Lester)*

NFH 120P undertaking Continental duties following its more arduous days on the Middle East run. The VIJORE NGCs continued with European work, hauling flat-bed trailers and curtain-siders as well as the usual tilts of the period.

Mike Beard, one of Richard Read's fitters at the time, reports that the two Tony Jones units (NFH 120P and PDF 444R) eventually joined the Read fleet. Mike remembers the Richard Read premises at Longhope as being like one big social club in those days, where the local lads stayed on in the evenings to finish whatever work was in hand before repairing to the pub together.

*(Photo: Marcus Lester)*

This rather poignant photograph was taken in the Richard Read 'graveyard' on their premises. The unit in front is NFH 120P, which had a Cummins 290 with a 13-speed Fuller; and the one behind is KFH 250P Cummins 335 with a 9-speed Fuller. Both did Middle East work to far-flung corners of the Wholly Lorriable Empire!

It appears that this vehicle was yet another NGC on the Middle East run. Writing in the August 1990 issue of *REVS* magazine (no. 11), its owner, John Simmons, wrote that when he bought it from Beech's Garage in Hanley, 'I was told that the ERF ran mainly from Stoke-on-Trent with tiles and tyres to the Middle East, returning with carpets and furniture to Glasgow, and was serviced after every trip at Beech's Garage. This model was definitely one of the best built by ERF.' He went on to explain that it had a Fuller 9-speed 'box and a Cummins NTC 335 which failed (broken crankshaft) and was replaced by another from a Ford Transcontinental. That too failed (slight head cracking) and was replaced by another ERF NGC bought for scrap in Belgium, along with a 13-speed Fuller to replace the original 9-speed (the story of which appears in the first book). A Rockwell drive axle was fitted in 1989.

*(Photos: John Simmons)*

GEH 513N is seen here on heavy haulage work. Bearing the chassis number 28658, it started life in 1974 with Albert Dale who sub-contracted for Beresford Transport of Tunstall doing round trips to Switzerland. It was presented in Beresford's own livery. The turbocharged 335 bhp-powered unit then passed on to John Simmons Heavy Haulage. It survived long enough to join the show circuit but it was eventually scrapped. The following advert was placed in the April 1994 issue of *REVS* magazine, which bore a photo of it on the front cover:

> For Sale. 'European' 4x2 tractor unit registered GEH 513N, due to lack of time to do this rare vehicle justice. This is a one off vehicle requiring very little mechanical work, but would require a good panel beater on the cab. The engine has never been driven at over 1600rpm for any time, apart from hill climbing, since fitted. It is in need of considerable restoration work.

I am reliably informed by John Heath, who briefly drove it, that the other ERF NGC in the livery of Beresford Transport was actually owned and

*(Photo: Jerry Cooke collection)*

operated by them on French plates from Le Havre with a regular French driver. It had a Cummins 335 and 9-speed Fuller. Later this vehicle went to Trans Arabia in Jeddah with the fleet number 125 and it appears in both liveries in *Lorries of Arabia*.

This unit, chassis number 27979, was operated by De Meulemeester of Pittem in Belgium. It became the donor vehicle for GEH 513N, which eventually acquired its NTC 335 engine, 13-speed gearbox, Jake Brake and rear suspension.

*(Photo: John Simmons)*

*(Photo: John Simmons)*

# ERF NGCS ON THE ARABIAN PENINSULA DOING 'INTERNALS'

Trans Arabia was the result of a partnership between S. Jones of Aldridge and Bin Zagr of Jeddah, Saudi Arabia. Trans Arabia had 12 NGCs in Jeddah during the '70s and early '80s, making it the largest-known operator of ERF NGCs. It ran other ERF models besides, in addition to Macks and Kenworths. Many of them ran as road-trains across the desert hauling two semi-trailers at gross weights up to 100 tonnes. This is the logo that adorned their cab doors.

In *Lorries of Arabia* many pages were devoted to the operator Trans Arabia. However, there is plenty more to say about this Jeddah-based fleet.

Just looking at these pictures, one of the first things I notice is the intensity of that Middle East light and the darkness of the shadows. Were any palm trees present, the drivers might well have squinted

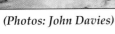
*(Photos: John Davies)*

47

at the sunlight streaming from the palm fronds like wet silver as they planned their recovery of this mishap in the desert. The vehicle facing is Trans Arabia fleet no. 142 which had a Cummins NTC 335 and a 9-speed Fuller gearbox. This was originally Eric Vick's KFH 248P, which had done some years of UK to Middle East work before arriving in Jeddah to do 'internals'. The other NGC, no. 126, was an ex-Dutch unit with a Cummins NTC 290 and a Fuller 13-speed gearbox.

No. 126, along with no. 124 (which had a Cummins 335/9-speed Fuller), was bought second-hand from Holland. Vince Cooke told me he picked them both up from Harwich docks on a flat-bed trailer. Of course, they rode high that day, but the only casualty was an orange beacon that was clobbered by an overhanging branch!

*(Photos: Mick Jones)*

As reported in more detail in the first book, Trans Arabia often ran their ERF NGCs with two semi-trailers and a dolly (one pictured) as 'road-trains', often at very high weights across the mountains and deserts of the Arabian Peninsula. Ken Broster, director and general manager of Trans Arabia in Jeddah, reports that although Trans Arabia's NGCs were generally reliable, they were prone to water-pump failures and troublesome needle bearings in the Kirkstall hub-reduction equipment.

Life was tough if you were attending to stranded ERFs in the desert. Trans Arabia mechanic Ron Hawkins was impressed with the ERFs and thought that the Cummins engines were brilliant, describing them as reliable and strong. He commented as follows:

> With good preventive maintenance these engines would outlive most if you paid particular attention to the desert dust! This was very obvious when you tipped the cab over and the sand came through the fan blades. It polished the front of the rocker cover and the timing case silver. The headlamp glass became frosted.

Ron observed that the Cummins sealing of all breathing parts was excellent. Filter changes were vital though. Injectors could be unblocked in situ, wherever the vehicle was stranded.

> In the sun the chrome spanners got too hot to handle so we kept them in petrol to keep them cool. We never used gloves! We just had on boots and shorts with a leather belt that turned grey with the salt. The scalding engine oil came out like water. We looked like scabby monkeys from the splashes where the sand stuck to the hot oil.

The chassis frame had to be strong too for ERFs shuddering along the shifting, shimmering shore-line sands of the Gulf on Trans Arabia work. It was made from manganese steel and was designed to absorb and distribute the heavy stresses that constantly occurred when carrying capacity (and more than capacity) loads, contributing greatly to the long-life reputation of ERF vehicles. All frame members and locating brackets were bolted, allowing every part to be easily replaced when major repair work was done.

This robust big-capacity 14-litre straight-six diesel engine design was brilliant. Even though it preceded after-cooled big cam versions with high torque at low revs, was under stressed, heavy, over engineered and thirsty, it was nonetheless turbocharged. Coupled to a Fuller gearbox and a Jacobs Brake in these trans-continental ERFs, the Cummins NTC 335 proved to be a highly durable, trouble-free, strong and resilient

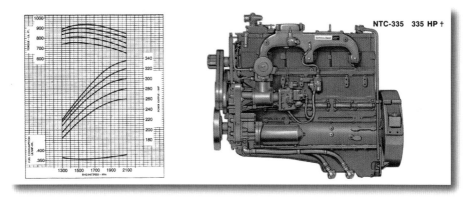

engine. History certainly appears to be on the side of this particular power plant.

These pictures give a hint of what life doing Saudi 'internals' with ERF NGCs was like. In the picture showing a container being unloaded from the front, Trans Arabia's kitchen lad, Ali, is seen on the left; whilst next to him stands the chauffeur, who sorted out

*(Photos: Mick Jones)*

any paperwork problems. The picture of drivers attending to the needs of one of their NGCs shows, from left to right, Trans Arabia drivers Billy Clem, Micky Jillings and 'Gypsy' Dave Anslow (incidentally, it gave me great pleasure to sign Gypsy Dave's copy of *Lorries of Arabia*!). Morning checks could be carried out by raising the front grille.

In addition to Trans Arabia, there were two other companies running local ERF NGCs out of Jeddah. One was Falcon Freight. In addition to the five NGCs supplied to Falcon Freight in Dubai, it now transpires that a further five were supplied to Jeddah, where they hauled flat-bed trailers carrying bagged cement. These had unusually long wheel-bases for tractive units, at 5.34 metres. The last of these units to be supplied to Falcon Freight, chassis number 31927, was also the last ever ERF with an MW cab and it was despatched on 22 December 1977. Unusually, it had a Cummins NTC E290 engine, matched to a Fuller RT 9509A gearbox.

It is also known that at least two NGCs (335s with 9-speed Fullers) were operated by Cunard Arabian Middle East Lines (CAMEL) in Jeddah; but an article in *Motor Transport* of 7 July 1978 states that 'Cunard operates a number of steel-cabbed ERF export-model tractors with Cummins NTC 335 engines for such work,' so clearly there were more than two.

One of Trans Arabia's ERF NGCs is seen here unloading a boat in the Jeddah. Although the bulk of their work was shipping-containers, Trans Arabia also undertook general haulage including boats and caravans across the peninsula from Jeddah to the Gulf. Ken Broster recalls that the

*(Photo: John Davies)*

local agent for this work was al-Quarashi. Routes included the TAP-line road (Trans Arabian Pipe) and the gruelling mountain route via Riyadh.

I asked Jerry Cooke, who drove and worked on NGCs in Jeddah, why S. Jones didn't operate on the Middle East run to the Gulf. He told me that they had sent some lorries overland to their operation in Jeddah (Trans Arabia), but that they had experienced a lot of setbacks and problems. Jerry said: 'If they had persevered with it I'm quite sure that they would have used a number of ERF NGCs on those routes because they were so reliable. Wonderful thing, hindsight, isn't it!'

*(Photos: Mick Jones)*

The photo above shows Jimmy Wells and Ron Hawkins twixt a brace of ERF NGCs on Trans Arabia work. The other picture shows Billy Clements and Kenny Jillings. Ron Hawkins was a mechanic for Trans Arabia and he produced the following account of the tough conditions.

I'm just remembering all our lads who drove in Saudi from the Persian Gulf across the yellowish sands in the east, past the red sands in the middle towards Riyadh; or to the mountain roads along the west coast from Jeddah to the Yemen border. They deserve to be praised: 44 degrees in the shade near Dammam driving south with no air-con. The hot wind made your ears burn. With D10 bulldozers continually pushing back sand dunes that had crossed the Abquac road and with the ruts in the road it was difficult enough keeping out of the line of fire from oncoming trucks. Shimmering heat made it look as if you were driving through vast lakes that blended into the sky, with no horizon, but in reality you were in the middle of the desert: it was unreal.

From Jeddah to the top of Taif Mountain was a slow drive but pretty safe at night. With only one way traffic it was all low gear and never flat out. Reaching the top there was a good parking area where you could rest up and meet your fellow truckers – maybe Johnny Longhorn with his bowl of water and towel on the bonnet trying to keep cool. Driving along this mountain road going south, the further you went the more your skills were called for. The Fuller Road-Ranger was the right 'box for this terrain: 350 miles of steep down-grades, sheer drops, 'tonkers' coming on strong and loaded to the gunnels with cement: no wonder there were wrecks everywhere. You could see they were overloaded and following them at night they swayed with their weight, climbing the mountain tops as they passed skull and cross-bones signs! You'd find somewhere to park up, only to move on again because the wind blew out the primus stove. This road only got worse. Still, red hot JP did well to stop his Mack before he lost it. That Mack was a bit agricultural compared to our ERFs!

Coming in from Dammam to Nazran in the south west with 800 miles of red hot desert, the temperature can soar to 48 plus. Breakdowns out there were challenging to say the least: repairs to trucks, heavy trailers on their knees, blow-outs and clutch and brake burn-outs all told their own stories. Even the spanners got too hot to handle. There were no air guns, no phones, no hotels, no shade, no cafes and no crumpet! Going from Khamis Nazran to Jizan, the mountains were nearly twice as high as Taif. These men earned their salt.

Ken Broster recalls that unaccompanied Unispeed 'fridge trailers were shipped into Jeddah on the *Seaspeed Dora*. These were tandem-axle, 12-metre 'fridge trailers loaded with Wall's products, including ice-cream. Bin Zagr, S. Jones's partner in the Trans Arabia concern, was the Saudi sales agent for all Unilever products. However, no

*(Photo: Mick Jones)*

onward distribution was undertaken by these trailers because the 'fridge motors were not reliable enough. They were fine aboard ship where they could be plugged into the vessel's electrics, but once on the docks awaiting customs clearance they needed checking at two-hour intervals. Apparently, they regularly stopped working. Once they had cleared customs they were taken straight to Bin Zagr's cold stores in Jeddah, or if they were shipped into Dammam they went to the cold store there. Ken recalls the following incident:

> We also did an overland stock shipment from Dammam to Jeddah. I was in Dammam when it left and I flew back to Jeddah that night. At lunchtime the next day the driver, a Philipino, walked in. I looked at him and said, 'That was quick driving!' He replied that the 'fridge had broken down in Riyadh so he just drove non-stop. It was repaired in minutes and the load was saved.

There were some pretty hairy mountain hills to be negotiated at high train weights in Saudi Arabia. To ensure long life and reliability, the NGCs were fitted with brakes with large brake lining areas, robust construction and attention to cooling. The three independent braking systems gave that security. In addition to the service brakes, NGCs were fitted with Jacobs Brakes.

The diagram shows the workings of a Jacobs Brake, more commonly known as a 'Jake Brake'. It was an early secondary braking system that slowed the engine down. This superb invention was fitted to all NGCs as standard equipment; and coupled with the Fuller 9-speed gearbox with which fast upshifts could be effected, meant that the NGC could out-perform other contemporary trucks in the mountains simply because it could go both up and down steep hills more quickly.

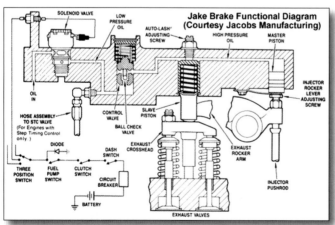

Jake Brake Functional Diagram
(Courtesy Jacobs Manufacturing)

# ERF NGCS IN CONTEXT: CONTEMPORARY ERF MODELS ON MIDDLE EAST WORK

*(Photo: Marcus Lester collection)*

Several ERF models were being made contemporaneously with the NGC. This picture shows a rare and invaluable juxtaposition of an ERF 5MW cab with a 7MW cab, both apparently on Middle East work, the 7MW-cabbed NGC in Richard Read livery and the 5MW-cabbed unit in VIJORE livery. Although the picture is indistinct, the visual differences between the two are clearly apparent. The VIJORE group ran 5MW-cabbed ERFs on Middle East work, one of which was HDF 228N which had RHD; and Trans Arabia operated two LHD examples with Cummins NTC 335s and 9-speed Fullers on 'internals'. Another LHD 5MW was photographed in Baghdad, also on 'internals', with the UK number GFH 727N. Others include a batch of 4MW-cabbed units hauling tankers in Doha, and even earlier 4MWs that were sent out to Jordan Phosphate Mines in the late '60s in large numbers – all LHD.

*(Photo: Ashley Coghill collection)*

The VIJORE group also ran A-series ERFs with the 7LV cab on Middle East work, in both Eric Vick and Richard Read liveries. Jennings sleeper pods were added. The one pictured had a Cummins 250 and a Jake Brake. Its day-cab was converted to a full sleeper and you can see this in the earlier photo taken from the Harem Hotel in Istanbul. Trans Arabia had two A-series units in Jeddah and some older LV-cabbed units. Earlier LV-cabbed units had also plied the overland routes, such as Euro-Asia's example which ran to Pakistan and one registered UTR 437H which managed three Kuwait trips with a 150 bhp Gardner. The odd-looking thing on the top of the NGC is simply an air-conditioner unit with its cover on.

Another contemporary was the ERF B-series, which continued after NGCs ceased. The next photo illustrates how much higher the driver sat in the NGC. The B-series pictured was one of six LHD units with double-drive operated out of Jeddah by Cunard Arabian Middle East Lines (CAMEL) with Cummins 350s and 9-speed Fullers. They also ran two ERF NGCs with the Cummins 335/9-speed Fuller combination.

*(Photo: Ian Tyler)*

Trans Arabia ran several similar B-series units, along with Caravan Trucking, Star Commercials and Taseco of Dammam. Trans Arabia also ran four 4x2 LHD B-series units with Cummins 290s and 13-speed Fullers.

A small number of B-series units were also driven on the Middle East overland run, including Nick Bull's LHD unit (YRF 823S), Manadient's LHD unit (PNV 486V), GVH's LHD unit (WNR 987S) and John Hallaumy's T-reg LHD unit.
Later ERFs to be exported to the Middle East were C-series in the '80s in various guises (4x2, 6x4, day-cab, sleeper-cab), including a huge order of 330 for Taseco in Dammam.

# REVISED ERF NGC REGISTER

| My ID no. | Reg. No. | Country of origin plate | Known engine & gearbox | Livery/Co | pic? | Year | Axle config. | Comments |
|---|---|---|---|---|---|---|---|---|
| 001 | N O3 66 / 34 UB 99 / 91 99 HB (re-registered in '80) | NL | NTC 335 | Vermeulen, Nieuwerkerk a.d. Ijssel | y | '76 | 4x2 | Michelin men, air horn, beacon, uitzonderlijk vervoer plate |
| 002 | 05 17 FB | NL | NTC 335 | Vermeulen, Nieuwerkerk a.d. Ijssel | y | '75 | 4x2 | Beacon, Michelin men, 326PK bumper |
| 003 | 87 69 RB | NL | NTC 335 | Willemstein, Barendrecht (till '81); De Regt, Nieuwerkerk (till '82); Vermeulen, Nieuwerkerk | y | '76 | 4x2 | Was run in Goodkoop de Geus livery by Willemstein, then Nabek livery by De Regt |
| 004 | KFH 248P/ TA 142 | GB / KSA | NTC 335 / Fuller 9 | Eric Vick, Hardwicke; Trans Arabia, Jeddah (late '82) | y | '75 | 4x2 | Air-con, visor, UK – Middle East on bumper, twin breather pipes |
| 005 | KFH 249P/ TA 143 | GB / KSA | NTC 335 / Fuller 9 | Eric Vick, Hardwicke; Trans Arabia, Jeddah (late '82) | y | '75 | 4x2 | Air-con, visor, Middle East – UK on bumper, twin breather pipes |
| 006 | KFH 250P | GB | NTC 335 / Fuller 9 | Richard Read, Longhope | y | '75 | 4x2 | Striped bumper, air-con, TIR plate, visor, twin breather pipes |
| 007 | NFH 120P | GB | NTC 290 / Fuller 13 | Richard Read, Longhope; Vijore, Hardwicke | y | '75 | 4x2 | Pair of stone-guarded bottom spots, striped bumper later. |

| My ID no. | Reg. No. | Country of origin plate | Known engine & gearbox | Livery/Co | pic? | Year | Axle config. | Comments |
|---|---|---|---|---|---|---|---|---|
| 008 | PDF 444R | GB | Cummins 335; 9-sp Fuller | Vijore, Hardwicke; Shamara Heavy Haulage, Southampton | y | | 4x2 | Bottom spots, visor, beacon later |
| 009 | Q691 NTR | GB | | Shamara Heavy Haulage, Southampton; Raynor | y | '75 | 6x4 | Originally a 4x2 unit. Roof rack, wide load on bumper |
| 010 | 7DF 44 / KCH 95N | B / GB | Cummins 335; left factory with Fuller RT 9508A but supplied with 13-sp Fuller RTO9513 | Marcel Eyckmans, Betekom; M. Corbishley, Uttoxeter | y | 24th May '74 | 6x4 | Originally a 4x2 unit, chassis no 27271, Trilex wheels, stack, Fassi crane |
| 011 | JDF 132N / Trans Arabia 125 | GB / KSA | NTC 335 / Fuller 9 | Beresford, Stoke; Trans Arabia, Jeddah | y | '74 | 4x2 | Originally carried French reg. plates. |
| 012 | GEH 513N | GB | NTC 335 / Fuller 9, later Fuller 13 | Albert Dale / Beresford, Stoke; John Simmons | y | '74 | 4x2 | Chassis no. 28658, stack, twin breather pipes – did Middle East |
| 013 | | GB | | ERF, Sandbach demo/promo | y | | 4x2 | - |
| 014 | GDS 543N | GB | | Greer, Holytown | y | | 4x2 | Striped bumper |

| My ID no. | Reg. No. | Country of origin plate | Known engine & gearbox | Livery/Co | pic? | Year | Axle config. | Comments |
|---|---|---|---|---|---|---|---|---|
| 015 | HNV 59N | GB | E290 | Cummins, New Malden; Pountains, Sudbury; Redcap Transport, Newport | y | '74 | 4x2 | NGC 420 but with 290 big cam Cummins Chassis no. 29069 (for hospitality trailer) |
| 016 | 4644FX94 | F | | | y | | 4x2 | Draw-bar tilt |
| 017 | ZH 120 919 | CH | NTC 335 | H Burkhard, Zurich | y | '74 | 4x2 | visor |
| 018 | | CH | | (Swiss O/D) | y | | 4x2 | Blue above bumper corners |
| 019 | 7601RR91 | F | | (white and orange) | y | | 4x2 | - |
| 020 | 1557 PF89 | F | NTC 290 / Fuller 13 (9513) | R Collin Exploitation Foresterie, 89 Montillet | y | | 4x2 | still intact though derelict |
| 021 | DEA044 (no.21) | B | NTC 335/ Fuller 9 | Van Steenbergen, Arendonk | y | '75 | 4x2 | Visor |
| 022 | 324BO (no.10) | B | NTC 335/ Fuller 9 | Van Steenbergen, Arendonk | y | '73 | 4x2 | Visor |
| 023 | 1HY84 (no.16) | B | NTC 335 / Fuller 9 | Van Steenbergen, Arendonk | y | '74 | 4x2 | Visor |
| 024 | AFU615 (no.28, later 31) | B | NTC 335/ Fuller RTO 9509A | Van Steenbergen, Arendonk | y | '74 | 4x2 | Chassis no. 22993, visor |
| 025 | 134D8 (no.09) | B | NTC 335/ Fuller 9 | Van Steenbergen, Arendonk | y | '73 | 4x2 | Visor |

| My ID no. | Reg. No. | Country of origin plate | Known engine & gearbox | Livery/Co | pic? | Year | Axle config. | Comments |
|---|---|---|---|---|---|---|---|---|
| 026 | L423R (no.19) | B | NTC 335/ Fuller 9 | Van Steenbergen, Arendonk | y | '75 | 4x2 | Visor |
| 027 | Q824 RGC | GB | | Reliable Recovery Services, London; BFI Recovery Services | y | | 4x2 | Wrecker |
| 028 | Fleet no. TA 106 | KSA | NTC 290 / Fuller 13 | (New to) Trans-Arabia, Jeddah | y | | 4x2 | |
| 029 | Fleet no. TA 108 | KSA | NTC 290 / Fuller 13 | (New to) Trans-Arabia, Jeddah | y | | 4x2 | Air horn, striped bumper, Arab decorations. |
| 030 | Fleet no. TA 110 | KSA | NTC 290 / Fuller 13 | (New to) Trans-Arabia, Jeddah | y | | 4x2 | Air horns, air-con. |
| 031 | Fleet no. TA 126 | NL / KSA | NTC 290 / Fuller 13 | Trans-Arabia, Jeddah; (prob the Schaap unit) | y | | 4x2 | Plastic visor, air-con, TIR |
| 032 | Fleet no. TA 124 | NL / KSA | NTC 335 / Fuller 9 | Trans-Arabia, Jeddah | y | | 4x2 | Ex-NL |
| 033 | KDM 460N | GB | NTC 335 / Fuller 9 | ERF, Sandbach (Trans Europe test) | y | '75 | 4x2 | Visor, 335/9sp. |
| 034 | | B | NTC 335 / Fuller 13 | De Meule meester, Pittem | y | | 4x2 | Chassis No. 27979 |
| 035 | KFH 251P | GB | NTC 335 / Fuller 9 | Richard Read, Longhope | y | '75 | 4x2 | Visor, Kysor air-con. Later converted to RHD and received a B-series day-cab |

| My ID no. | Reg. No. | Country of origin plate | Known engine & gearbox | Livery/Co | pic? | Year | Axle config. | Comments |
|---|---|---|---|---|---|---|---|---|
| 036 | 12 97 FB /TA 139 | NL / KSA | NTC 335 / Fuller 9 | Groenenboom, Ridderkerk (till '77); Steef Slappendel; Trans Arabia | y | | 4x2 | Believed to have done Middle East run |
| 037 | 41 54 NB | NL | NTC 335 / Fuller 9 | Barend Sjouw, Poortugaal | y | '76 | 4x2 | Plastic visor, ex-demonstrator |
| 038 | Fleet no. TA 105 | KSA | NTC 290 / Fuller 13 | (New to) Trans Arabia, Jeddah | y | | 4x2 | |
| 039 | Fleet no. TA 109 | KSA | NTC 290 / Fuller 13 | (New to) Trans Arabia, Jeddah | y | | 4x2 | |
| 040 | 5673KH59 | F | NTC 335 / Fuller 9 | Loste, Hellemes-Lille | y | | 4x2 | |
| 041 | Fleet no. TA 107 | KSA | NTC 290 / Fuller 13 | (New to) Trans Arabia, Jeddah | y | | 4x2 | |
| 042 | | GB | | Comart | y | | 4x2 | |
| 043 | JJ393 | B | NTC 335 / Fuller RTO909A | Thibaut, Stree (ex-ERF demo) | y | '73 | 4x2 | Drawbar outfit Chassis no. 24684 Engine 51900 |
| 044 | JLG 35N | GB | | ERF, Sandbach demo | y | '74 | 4x2 | Air-con, visor, breather pipes |
| 045 | 2751W?? | F | | Laiteries Preval, Vire | y | | 4x2 | |
| 046 | MMG 772P | GB | | | y | '75 | 4x2 | unsignwritten |
| 047 | 7650DA93 | F | | | y | '74 | 4x2 | unsignwritten |
| 048 | 7011KG78 | F | | Mentre, Yvelines | y | '74 | 4x2 | |

| My ID no. | Reg. No. | Country of origin plate | Known engine & gearbox | Livery/Co | pic? | Year | Axle config. | Comments |
|---|---|---|---|---|---|---|---|---|
| 049 | 8814GV59 | F | NTC 335 / Fuller 9 | Loste, Hellemes-Lille | y | '75 | 4x2 | |
| 050 | 3987RM50 | F | | | y | '75 | 4x2 | unsignwritten |
| 051 | 813AMH75 | F | | | y | '75 | 4x2 | Did Middle East work |
| 052 | DB 77 52 | NL | | Kooij, Hendrik-Ido-Ambacht; Willemstein, Barendrecht | y | '74 | 4x2 | Completed 1.3 million kms before being sold to a breaker in 1989 still in HT Wilhelminakade livery |
| 053 | 16 37 FB | NL | | Groen, Nieuw Lekkerland (till '82) | y | '75 | 4x2 | |
| 054 | 83 75 HB | NL | NTC 335 | Rien De Vos, Goudswaard (till '79) | y | '76 | 4x2 | 440,000 kms on the clock: no major probs |
| 055 | 21 96 NB | NL | NTC 335 | Rien De Vos, Goudswaard (till '80) | y | '76 | 4x2 | |
| 056 | X 03 44/ 84-56-JB | NL | | Schaap, Rotterdam; (prob TA 126) | y | '76 | 4x2 | Ben Schaap later ran it in the livery of Konig |
| 057 | 06 09 TB | NL | | Groenenboom, Ridderkerk | y | '77 | 4x2 | |
| 058 | | UAE | NTC 335 | Falcon Freight, Dubai | y | '75/6 | 4x2 | |
| 059 | | UAE | NTC 335 | Falcon Freight, Dubai | y | '75/6 | 4x2 | |
| 060 | | UAE | NTC 335 | Falcon Freight, Dubai | y | '75/6 | 4x2 | |
| 061 | | UAE | NTC 335 | Falcon Freight, Dubai | y | '75/6 | 4x2 | |
| 062 | | UAE | NTC 335 | Falcon Freight, Dubai | y | '75/6 | 4x2 | |

| My ID no. | Reg. No. | Country of origin plate | Known engine & gearbox | Livery/Co | pic? | Year | Axle config. | Comments |
|---|---|---|---|---|---|---|---|---|
| 063 | KRH 153P | GB | NTC 335 / Fuller 9; then Cummins 350 / Fuller 13 /coach diff | PG Horridge, Poole | y | | 4x2 | TIR-plate, visor |
| 064 | | B | | | y | | 4x2 | CDB demonstrator. Red with white band |
| 065 | 8264RW95 | F | | Cauvas, Bonneuil en France | y | '75 | 6x4 | NGC 852 |
| 066 | | KSA | NTC 335 / Fuller 9 | CAMEL, Jeddah | y | | 4x2 | |
| 067 | | KSA | NTC 335 / Fuller 9 | CAMEL, Jeddah | y | | 4x2 | |
| 068 | | F | | Transports Gentilucci Freres, Villeneuve La Garenne | y | | 4x2 | Draw-bar tilt |
| 069 | BFN-379? | B | | Transports Gruwez, Brugge | y | | | Red plastic visor |
| 070 | HMO-220N | GB | | Calor | y | | 4x2 | |
| 071 | | KSA | | Falcon Freight, Jeddah | | '75/6 | 4x2 | 5.34m w/b |
| 072 | | KSA | | Falcon Freight, Jeddah | | '75/6 | 4x2 | 5.34m w/b |
| 073 | | KSA | | Falcon Freight, Jeddah | | '75/6 | 4x2 | 5.34m w/b |
| 074 | | KSA | | Falcon Freight, Jeddah | | '75/6 | 4x2 | 5.34m w/b |

| My ID no. | Reg. No. | Country of origin plate | Known engine & gearbox | Livery/Co | pic? | Year | Axle config. | Comments |
|---|---|---|---|---|---|---|---|---|
| 075 | | KSA | Cummins NTC E290 / Fuller RT 9509A | Falcon Freight, Jeddah | | Dec 1977 | 4x2 | Chassis no. 31927. Last ever ERF MW 5.34m w/b |
| 076 | 785AHD75 | F | | | y | | | |
| 077 | | NL | | Damco / Goedkoop – De Geus | | | | |
| 078 | | GB | | ERF | | | | Demo for S Jones: written off in an accident. This may be 041 (TA107) which was supplied new with accident damage |

# BIBLIOGRAPHY

*Lorries of Arabia: ERF NGC* by Robert Hackford; Old Pond Publishing 2015
*TRUCK* magazine June 1975
*TRUCK* magazine July 1975
*TRUCK* magazine January 1976
*TRUCK* magazine July/August 1977
*TRUCK* magazine July 1978
*TRUCKING* magazine Summer (July) 2015
*Commercial Motor* magazine 12 May 1984
*Chassis* magazine no. 20
*REVS* magazine April 1994 no. 32
*REVS* magazine August 1990 no. 11
*Motor Transport* magazine 7 July 1978

*This ERF demonstrator was fully equipped for the Middle East run, complete with Kysor, visor and breather pipes, though it is not known whether or not the unit ever left these shores. The excellent picture was taken by Alan Rickett who was ERF's publicity photographer for many years. It is worthy of note that the unusual semi-trailer appears to be an ERF demonstrator too. (c) Alan Rickett*